ALPHABET

Words by Robin Feiner

A is for Tony **A**rmas.
A big hitter in the middle of the '80s lineup, Armas smashed home runs and led the league in 1981 and '84. He helped the Red Sox reach the 1986 World Series and became one of the team's power stars.

B is for Bobby Doerr.
Quiet, steady, and strong —
Bobby Doerr was the heart of
the Red Sox for nearly 14 years.
He was a Hall of Fame second
baseman who made fielding
look easy and hitting look
smooth.

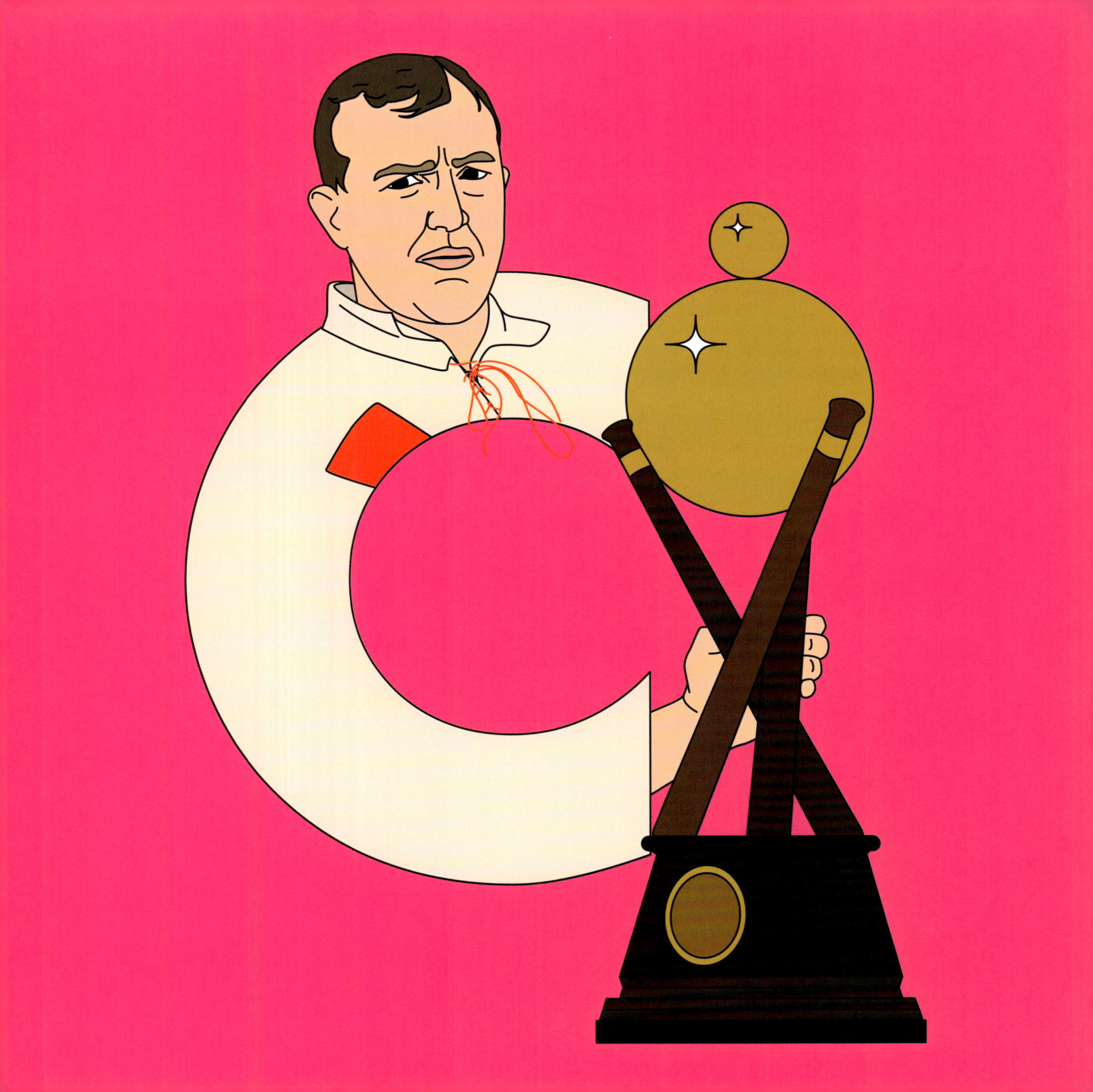

C is for Cy Young.
The man, the legend, and the name on baseball's most famous pitching award. Cy Young brought speed and skill to the mound long before modern pitchers.

D is for **D**wight Evans.
'Mr. Reliable' in the outfield,
Dewey Evans had a strong arm
and a bat that came alive when
it mattered. He won eight Gold
Gloves and became a Fenway
favorite.

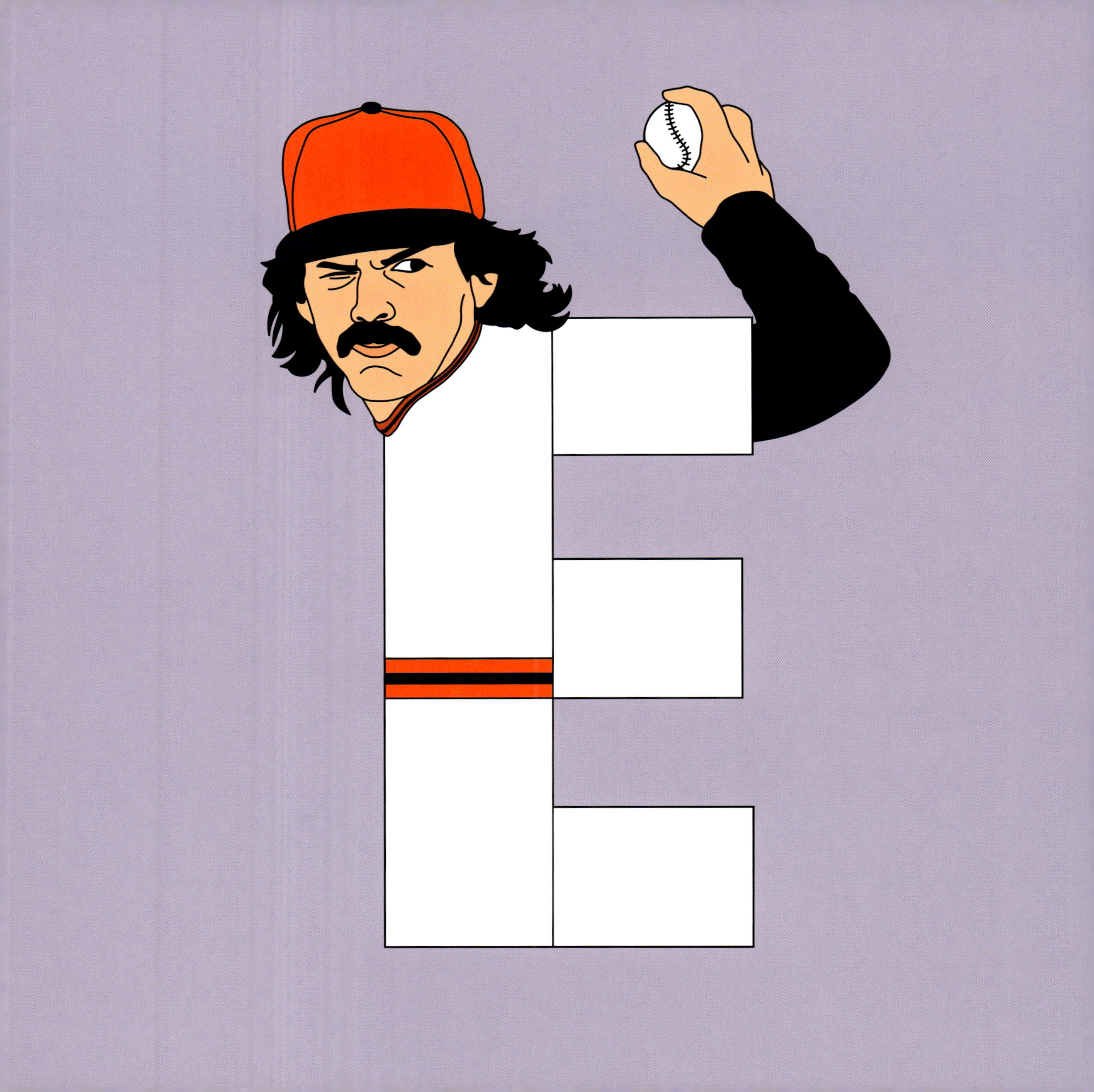

E is for Dennis Eckersley. Before the cool glasses and big saves in Oakland, 'Eck' began his story in Boston. He pitched with power and confidence — and went on to inspire pitchers everywhere.

Ff

F is for **F**red Lynn.
Fred Lynn made baseball magic in 1975, winning both MVP and Rookie of the Year. He flew through the outfield and hit balls over the Green Monster.

Gg

G is for George 'Duffy' Lewis. Before the Green Monster even had a name, Duffy ruled left field. He starred in three World Series and helped form the 'Golden Outfield.'

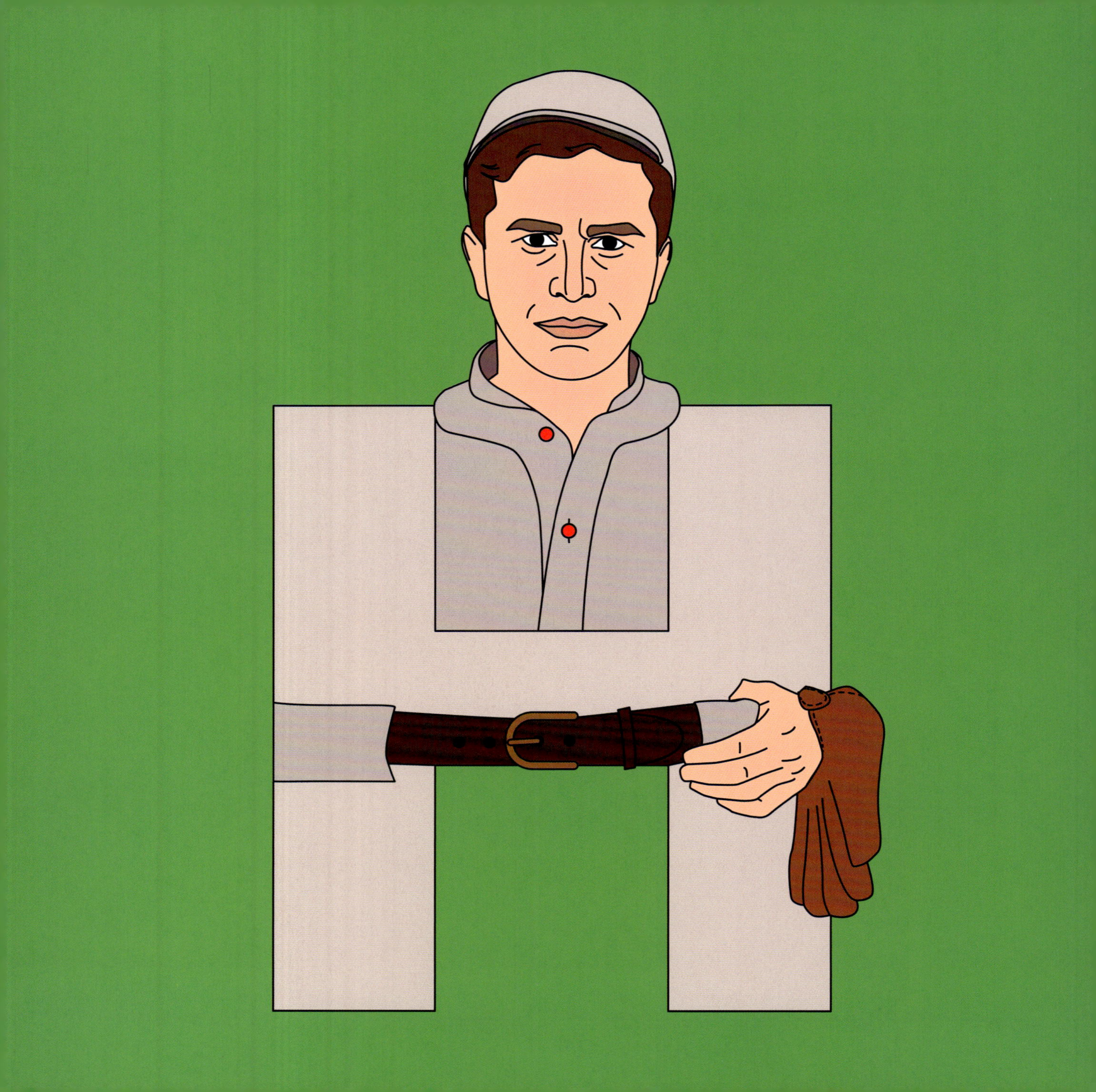

Hh

H is for Harry Hooper.
Four World Series championships.
A Hall of Fame spot. And a big
role in the Red Sox's early days.
Harry Hooper helped build
Boston's baseball story from
the start.

Ii

I is for Ike Delock.
A dependable pitcher through the 1950s, Ike kept batters guessing with his curveball and calm control. He spent over a decade in Boston, becoming a steady force on the mound.

J is for Jim Rice.
Strong, fearless, and ready to hit. Jim Rice was one of the most powerful batters of his time and a Red Sox legend for years.

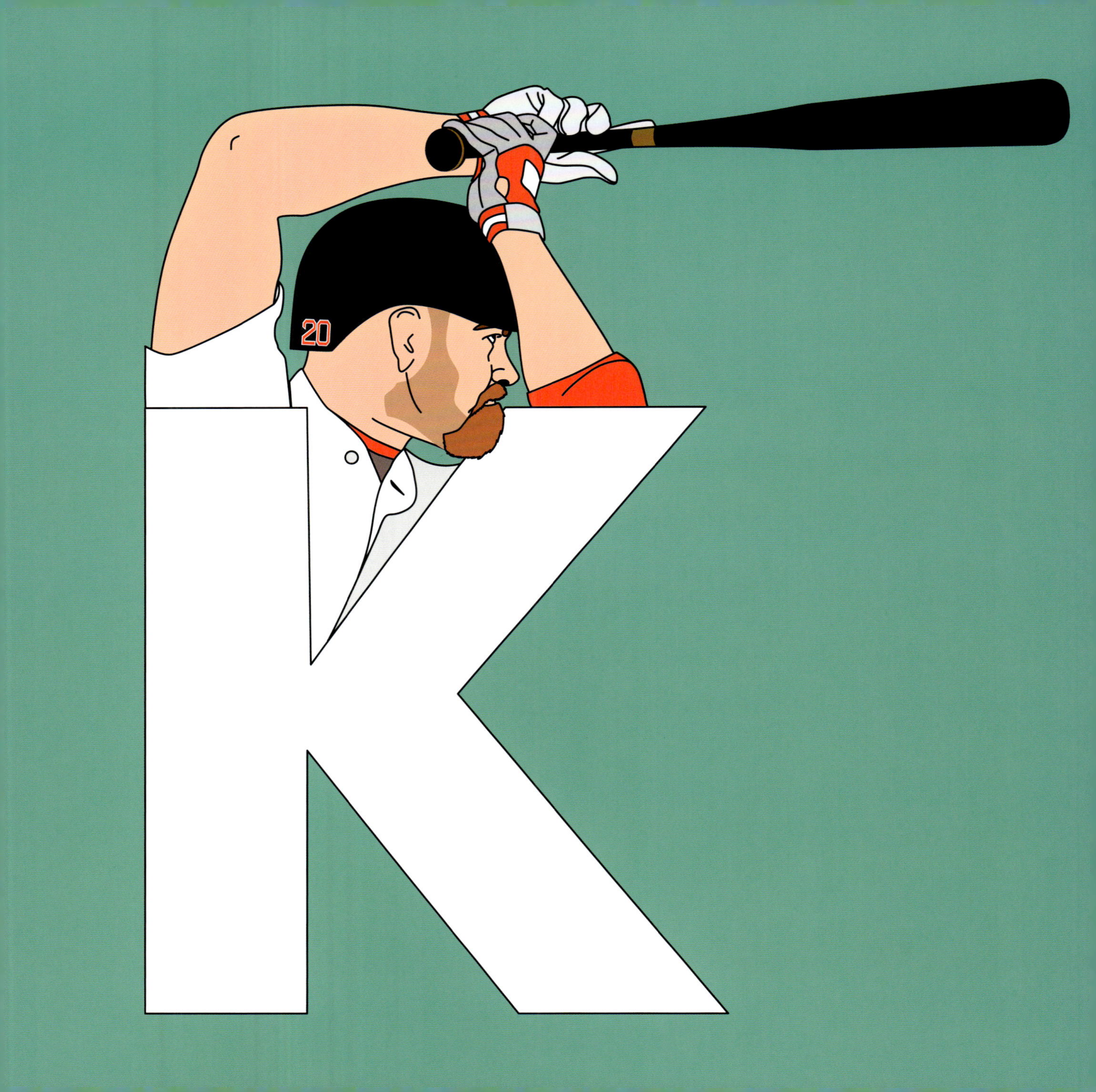
K
20

K is for **K**evin Youkilis.
The 'Greek God of Walks'
turned patience into power.
With his funny stance and fiery
play, Youk became a fan
favorite and a two-time
World Series champ.

L is for Jon Lester.
Jon fought cancer and came back even stronger. He ruled the mound and helped the Red Sox win two World Series—with ice in his veins.

M is for Pedro **M**artínez.
Fast. Fierce. Fun to watch. Pedro ruled the late '90s with blazing fastballs and a fearless pitching style. When he pitched, Fenway went wild.

Nn

N is for **N**omar Garciaparra. With his batting gloves just right, Nomar wowed the fans at Fenway in the late '90s. A two-time batting champ and shortstop star, he was loved by fans before the curse was broken.

O is for David Ortiz.
Big Papi came up big — again and again. From walk-off hits to three World Series wins, Ortiz's clutch plays and big heart made him a Boston hero.

P
15

P is for Dustin **P**edroia.
Small in size, huge in heart.
'Pedey' played with dirt on
his jersey and fire in his soul—
winning awards and helping
the Red Sox bring home two
World Series trophies.

1918 BELIEVE 2004
BELIEVE
FINALLY!
THANK
RED
YOU
SOX

Q is for Quest for the Championship. For 86 years, Red Sox fans waited. Then came the heroes of 2004, ending the curse and starting a new winning story. The quest was finally complete.

Rr

R is for Babe Ruth.
Before becoming a Yankee star, Babe Ruth was a Red Sox pitcher — and a great one. He helped Boston win three World Series before the biggest trade in baseball history.

S is for Smoky Joe Wood.
In 1912, Smoky Joe threw fireballs — winning 34 games and the World Series. He was Boston's first pitching superstar.

T

Tt

T is for Ted Williams.
The greatest hitter who ever lived. Ted Williams saw the ball like no one else — and gave everything he had to the game and his country.

U is for the Ultimate Comeback. Down 3–0 to the Yankees in 2004, the Red Sox did the impossible. Four wins in a row. A miracle. The greatest comeback in baseball history.

V
C
33
33

V is for Jason Varitek.
The captain. The mask. The leader of the team. Varitek led by example and caught for some of the best pitchers in Red Sox history.

W is for Tim Wakefield.
He threw knuckleballs and won hearts. Wakefield pitched with kindness, loyalty, and a pitch that danced through the air.

X

X is for Xander Bogaerts.
Calm and powerful, Xander
helped win two World Series.
He was a smooth shortstop
with a world-class swing.

Yy

Y is for Carl Yastrzemski.
Yaz was the pride of Fenway Park for over two decades. A Triple Crown winner and team captain, he gave everything to the game — and then some.

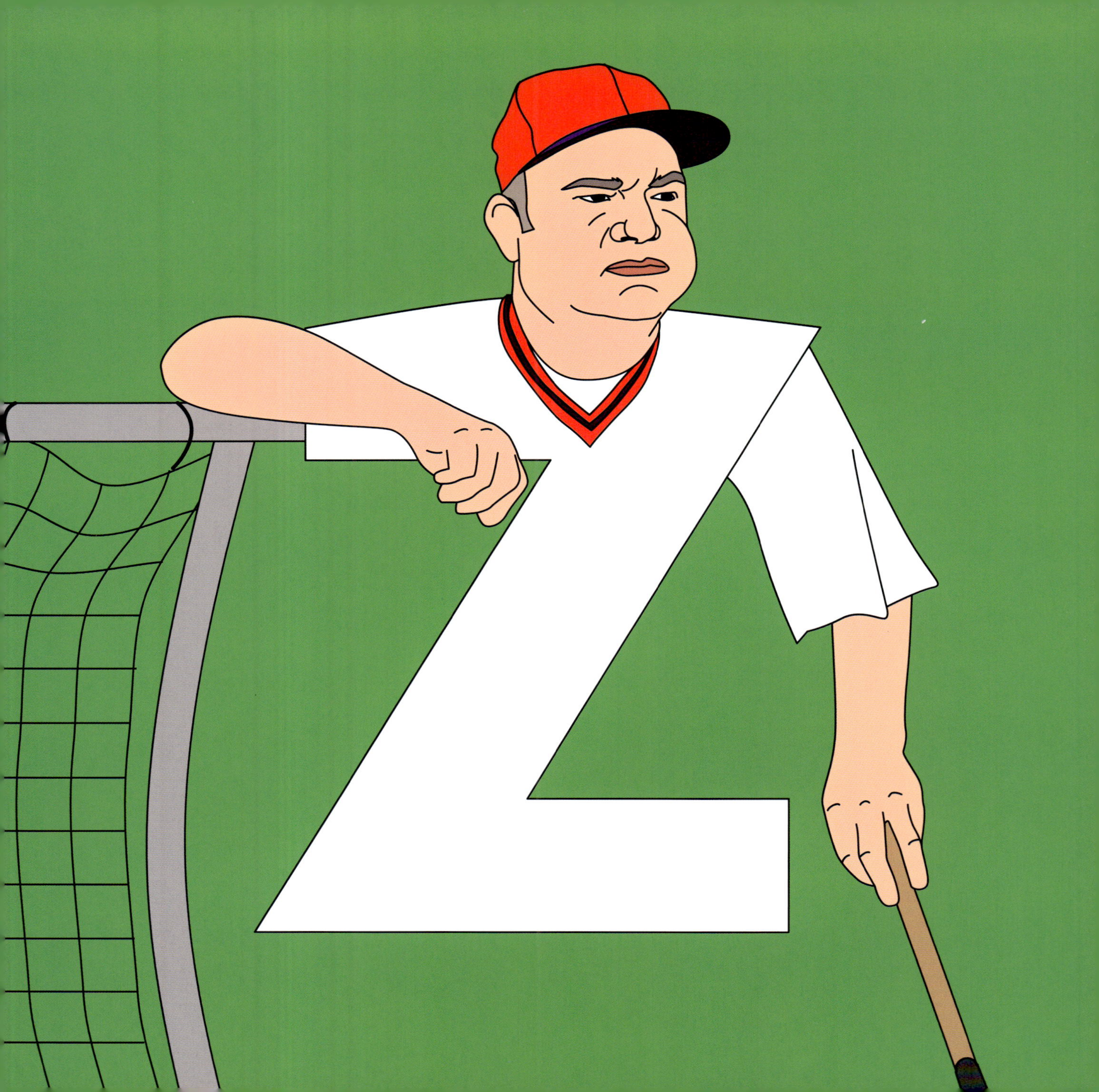
Z

Zz

Z is for Don Zimmer.
Zim was a baseball lifer — player, manager, and coach. His Red Sox years were full of passion, grit, and loyalty to the game he loved.

The ever-expanding legendary library

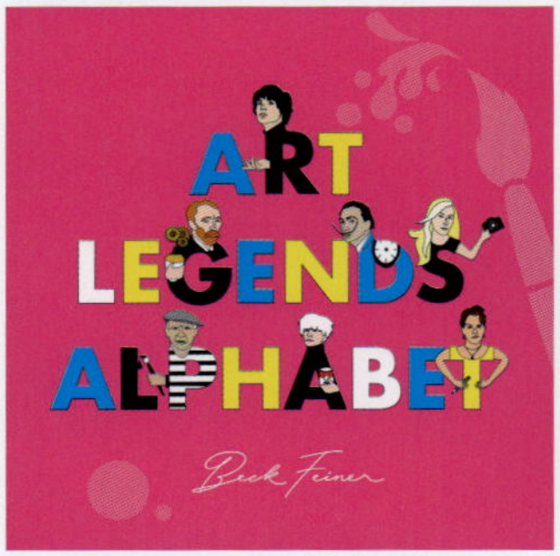

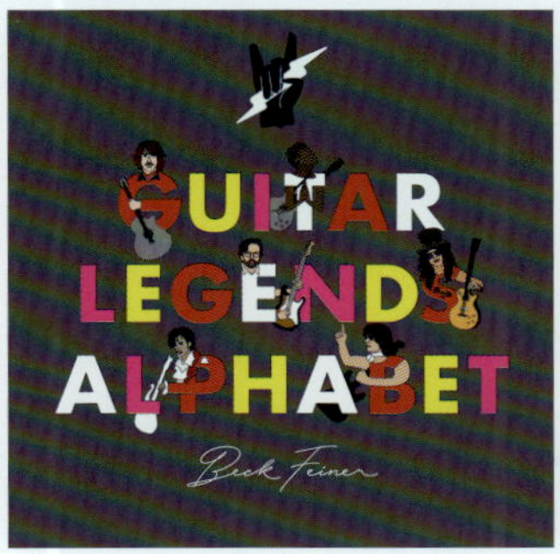

EXPLORE THESE LEGENDARY ALPHABETS & MORE AT WWW.ALPHABETLEGENDS.COM

RED SOX ALPHABET
www.alphabetlegends.com

Published by Alphabet Legends Pty Ltd in 2025
Created by Beck Feiner

Printed and bound in China.

9781763865235

ALPHABET LEGENDS